Chakras

The Chakra Theory: Investigating The Energy Centers
Located Within The Human Body And The Holistic
Effects They Have On A Person's Physical And Spiritual
Well-Being

Colin Archer

TABLE OF CONTENT

Introduction 1

The Essential Blunder That Nearly All People Commit 7

"Anahata" Is The Name Of The Heart Chakra, Which Is Located Inside The Heart 9

What Exactly Are The Chakras? 20

A Sacral Chakra That Is Both Open And Balanced 32

Crystal Healing 47

The Heart Chakra 57

The Chakra At The Crown 63

The Third Eye, Also Known As The Brow Chakra 74

Bringing Our Life Force Into Harmony And Purification 78

The Process Of Cleaning Your Chakras 83

Treatment With Reiki Is Effective For A Variety Of Illnesses 105

Chakra Guide 109

The Qualities That Are Associated With Each Chakra 115

Meditations With Chakra Mantras To Release Pent-Up Energy 120

Meditation On The Heart Chakra 145

Introduction

However, what exactly are chakras? Because of the way energy travels through the body, a Sanskrit word that translates to "wheel" may be used to refer to a chakra. Since we are talking about the body at the moment, please allow me to expand on the topic. Because of their resemblance to spinning wheels, the energy centers of the organization, which make up the bulk of the organization's structure, are often referred to as chakras. These energy vortices, known as chakras, are responsible for the flow of energy, which might begin in one zone and go on to the next. These energy centers, known as chakras, are inextricably linked to the day-to-day routine of living because of the strong connections that may be formed between sound, color, and light. In the process of healing, the goal is to balance the chakras by successfully altering them while also focusing on the crucial task of comprehending nature for what it is worth about creation and the function of the individuals in view.

The human body is structured to have a total of seven energy centers known as chakras. The main chakra, also known as the red chakra, is positioned exactly at the base of the spine. It is sometimes referred to as the root chakra because of its proximity to the base of the spine. The Kundalini chakra is another term for this particular chakra. The orange hue represents the second chakra, which is the spleen, and it is located just below the scar left by the umbilical cord. This chakra is the second of the seven chakras. The chakras become more active as a result of meditating, which indicates that the goal of balancing the chakras in order to reach the desired arrangement cannot be accomplished without the practice of meditation. Regardless of this, the second chakra is in charge of determining sexual boundaries, and if it becomes imbalanced, there is room for blame.

The third of the seven chakras is the sun-oriented plexus, which refers to the location of one's sentiments and is the source of the color yellow, which represents power on earth and this chakra. This chakra is located in the middle of the body. The color green represents the fourth chakra, which is also known as the heart chakra. This chakra is seen or manifested when there is a lack of empathy in the spirit, and it is referred to as the heart chakra. This emoji demonstrates the freedom to express one's mind even when practicing meditation. The throat chakra is associated with the color blue and is also known as the fifth chakra. The third eye chakra, which is the sixth chakra before we combine them all together to form the seven chakras, is symbolized by the color blue and always features the forehead as a vital component of these energy components.

The crown chakra is the seventh and last chakra, and its mission is to link you with higher realms. It is represented by the color purple, and it is the chakra that concludes the negotiations on the other seven chakras. Chakras are continually visible in the body because they are always absorbing energy while simultaneously increasing with color, light, and sound. Prana is the name given to the deep energy that flows forth from each of these chakras. Prana is absorbed by the chakra centers, which causes them to vibrate, ultimately leading to the delivery of power. When prana finally fuses with the brain, we will be able to say that the key goal of reducing the effects of imbalance in the chakras has been accomplished. This was the primary aim.

The astral body and the physical body are joined together via a link known as prana. Numerous questions about chakras may be answered via the practice of meditation. For instance, how does the energy get started, how does it get transported, and what are the advantages of doing so? If you have a genuine understanding of the advantages of yoga asana, you will understand that balancing the chakras is another opportunity to release the unstable energy that might cause one person to misjudge another's assessment of the actual world. This has, the majority of the time, been made clear in the course of astral explorations and astral investigations. The following is a list of the terminological words that are used to refer to the seven chakras: Mooladhara, Swadhisthana, Manipura, Anahata, Vishuddhi, Ajna, and Sahasrara. The purpose of these chakras is to reflect the individual's psychological condition and interpret it in relation to each energy center. Chakras may only be said to be in a condition of fundamental equilibrium if they are allowed to contract their vibration at a predetermined frequency. So, when their energy cannot flow, what do chakras become? When one of the chakras or energy centers is blocked, it has an effect on our physical welfare, which is why people start becoming sick when this happens.

At the end of the day, the energy centers that are the recovering states of these viewpoints are what we call energy centers. In traditional Hinduism, the energy centers, known as chakras in this context, are depicted in several forms of tantric teachings. These works are considered to be authoritative. However, in today's modern world, this idea is related with prana, and its origins may be traced back to the seventeenth century, when a well-known scientist used animal magnetism as a treatment for a particular illness. However, there has not yet been any scholarly investigation done on this mystery, despite the fact that the idea of chakras has been inextricably linked with the achievements of this scientist.

The Essential Blunder That Nearly All People Commit

The great majority of people, when they first start making an effort to develop their psychic potential, make the key error of not paying significant regard to the privilege chakras. This is the mistake that costs them the most ground. What exactly are the chakras? They are the points of concentration of energy in your brain and body that give you access to your intuitive faculties. They need to be set in stone and tweaked with the ultimate objective of making the most of your perceptive nature. The following are the three "super chakras" that are essential to the process of expanding your capabilities:

The Chakra at the Crown - The crown chakra is responsible for connecting us with the overall energy source that is all around us. It is situated at the very top of the head, at the highest position. This is the item that allows psychics to utilize their intuition to fuel their psychic skills. Psychics' talents are powered by their intuition.

The Brow Chakra is the chakra that is most often referred to as "the third eye." It is responsible for linking the conscious mind with the deepest levels of the subconscious mind. In order for a psychic to make use of their skills, the Brow Chakra has to be relaxed and open.

This chakra is in charge of your psychic ability and intuition. It is located in the heart. Your natural intellectual capacity is located in the centre of the structure. By rerouting your intuitive energy from your heart chakra to your crown chakra, you may unlock the extraordinary power that lies dormant within you.

"Anahata" Is The Name Of The Heart Chakra, Which Is Located Inside The Heart.

This chakra is associated with the kinesthetic sensation of touch. It is situated close to the plexus of the heart and influences a person's sense of self-identity, as well as their capacity to provide insight and love that is not conditional, as well as their capacity for patience and comparison. When this chakra is out of alignment, it has a negative impact on the upper back and the shoulders, and it may also lead to heart and lung ailments, asthma, and other respiratory disorders. There are also mental and emotional problems that might surround a person who does not have this chakra in a balanced state. Some examples of these problems are a lack of empathy and compassion, wrath and anxiety, and even envy. You have an empathetic sense, you are cheerful, and you are free of any animosity when this chakra is in a state of balance. Lavender and jasmine are two examples of essential oils that might help bring this chakra back into balance.

The heart chakra is the fourth chakra in the body. It causes the chakras to become disconnected from one another, and as a consequence, it often results in qualities that influence the individual's way of spirit. People that are defiant in this area are often reserved and lack empathy for others. They have a difficult time forgiving others, and as a result, they often feel angry and are unable to develop healthy ties with other people. This deficit may lead to a range of adverse impacts on a person's health, including difficulties with, among other things, the heart. High blood pressure, heart disease, and jealousy are all examples of disorders that are seen often. Backbends and the Eagle Pose are two of the suggested yoga positions for stimulating this chakra as part of your practice. Even while these things are helpful, the one that is most helpful and provides the most effective kind of rehabilitation is love, both the capacity to love and the ability to be loved.

The Anahata chakra is located in the middle of the chest and is responsible for regulating the functions of the lungs, blood, the circulatory system, the thymus, the diaphragm, the heart, the esophagus, the shoulders, the arms, the legs, and the breasts.

Compassion, forgiveness, passion, dedication, love for self and love for others, as well as your circulatory system, are all directly impacted by the heart chakra. If this chakra is out of balance, it may cause health problems such as lung cancer, pneumonia, breast cancer, shoulder difficulties, confidence issues, envy, fear, hatred, despair, confidence, passivity, and jealousy. Shoulder problems can also be caused by an imbalanced chest chakra.

Your energy is stored in the heart chakra, which is also known as the "heart of healing" and "the center of love." This energy area is linked to your emotions and gives you the ability to love and give without condition. In addition to this, it makes any necessary emotional healing easier to accomplish and acts as a link between your physical body and your spiritual self. When this chakra is activated and functioning properly, you will have a sense that you are linked to everyone in your life.

The Heart Chakra: The Ability to Love

The fourth chakra, also known as the heart chakra, is situated in the middle of the chest, directly above the heart. Its Sanskrit name is "Anahata," which translates as "unstruck" or "unhurt," and its location is directly above the heart. It is linked to the body's respiratory and circulatory systems via this connection.

This chakra represents the force of love, and it is connected to the processes of healing and maintaining health. The element of air serves as its foundation. It is the link that binds the mind, the body, the soul, and the emotions all together. The love, beauty, compassion, kindness, empowerment, and connection that we experience in our lives come from the heart chakra.

This chakra's energy is related to expansiveness as well as having a connection to everything in the universe. In spite of the fact that most people associate it with the color pink, its true meaning is really associated with the color green. The representation of a chakra consists of a circle with twelve petals, a triangle pointing downwards entwined with another triangle pointing upwards to form a six-pointed star or hexagram, and a triangle pointing upwards to complete the sign.

Put your sorrow at the forefront of your mind in order to restore harmony to the heart chakra. Spend some time giving your sentiments of loss and despair the respect and appreciation they deserve. This enlightens us to the fact that it is precisely the suffering that we experience in our lives that teaches us how to let go and forgive; when we are able to do so, we are in a position to love more deeply.

The Heart Chakra and Other Non-Traditional Methods of Healing

The color is green.

Air, the element

Localization: in the middle of the chest, directly over the heart

Ailments of the Emotions Caused by Blockages: Behaviors such as being antisocial and feeling lonely, having poor boundaries, being codependent, and concentrating too much on other people

Asthma, respiratory issues, feeling weary or worn out, severe skin problems, susceptibility to colds and coronary or circulation disorders are some examples of the physical ailments that may result from blockages.

Rose Quartz, Tsavorite garnet, watermelon tourmaline, rainbow fluorite, pink topaz, peridot, moss agate, mangano calcite, malachite, labradorite, jade, green apatite, fuchsite, eudialyte, emerald, aventurine, amazonite, and alexandrite are some of the crystals that may be used for healing with crystals.

Lemon balm, thyme, white horn, and other medicinal herbs include: A. Melissa

The Bach Method of Healing Willow, red chestnut, and chicory flowers are used in flower therapy.

Jasmine, rose, tarragon, and vanilla are some of the essential oils that may be used for healing.

Using sound to heal, chant the "YAM" sound, which is the universal seed sound.

Using affirmations to facilitate healing: "My heart is open to love." "I accept myself with kindness and compassion." "I give and receive with a heart that is open to all living beings,"

Listen to music that you like, wear the color green, have a massage, hug and comfort other people, connect with nature, and spend time outdoors are all great ways to activate the heart chakra.

Meditation and Yoga Pose: Fish Pose or the Cobra Pose

Throat Chakra: The ability to express oneself and to be heard

The fifth chakra, often known as the neck chakra, is sometimes referred to by its Sanskrit name, "Vishuddha," which literally translates to "pure." This chakra is associated with our capacity for communication and enables us to give expression to our innermost beliefs. The inspiration, sincerity, intellect, and creativity that come from this chakra are channeled via the throat. It is about expressing our truth and our purpose in life, which is a fundamental way of expression and communication in our culture.

The throat chakra is an etheric energy center that links humans to the spirit world. It sits in the exact middle of the neck and is perpendicular to the trachea (windpipe). The fact that it is situated at the neck gives it the reputation of being the "bottleneck" of the flow of energy throughout the body. When we open the throat chakra, we are able to better connect our vision with reality and release the pressure that might potentially have a detrimental effect on the heart chakra, which is located below it.

The color blue (also known as aquamarine or turquoise) is used to symbolize this chakra. A crescent with a circle contained inside it forms part of its symbol, which also has a circle within a circle. It is often shown as a circle inside of which is carved a triangle pointing in a downward direction. This triangle is contained inside another circle.

It is necessary to let go of our denial and the falsehoods that we tell ourselves in order to bring the throat chakra back into equilibrium. Our subconcious is able to see right through any justification or explanation that we provide. It is not possible for us to deceive either ourselves or the outside world on the essence of who we really are.

What Exactly Are The Chakras?

In India, there has been a well-developed tradition of studying the human body, as well as its vitality and potential, for thousands of years. Your body is made up of seven different centers, and those centers may be found dispersed all across the body. These centers form the body's energy foundation. You will be astounded at the effects that may be observed in both your day-to-day life and in all of the work that you do when you are able to align all of your energy centers. These results can be experienced in both areas simultaneously. Through the effective alignment of intent and purpose, you will have the ability to identify methods to concentrate your energy as well as to transcend your own obstacles to success in your pursuit of success.

A Brief Overview of Chakra History:

In the Western culture, the practice of meditation, as well as the tradition of really comprehending the requirements of the spiritual body, are relatively recent developments. Over 6,000 years ago in India, the tradition of Hinduism gave rise to yoga. Yoga was first practiced in India. It appears in the book as a reference to a means to be able to balance all of the energy in your body as well as a way to be able to connect with the universal energies that flow throughout the universe. Additionally, it refers to a technique to be able to connect with the energies that flow throughout the universe. It is believed that all of the energy in the cosmos may be tapped into via the body as it is transferred from one chakra to the next.

This is something that has been passed down through traditions and teachings. The original meaning of the term yoga, which derives from Sanskrit, is "union." The word "wheel" is where the term "chakra" originates from. This signified that all of the body's energies were constantly moving in a circular motion throughout the body, making it possible to channel all of these energies at the same time, allowing for the transmission of energy from one part of the body to another, as well as the concentration and channeling of energy for any purpose that may be necessary. Chakras can be found throughout the body.

According to the teachings of yoga, it is possible to flow energy in any direction and from one spot to another. There are in fact seven chakras that may be aligned from the head to the foot. It is believed that the alignment of the chakras runs directly in accordance to the seven stars that make up the Big Dipper, and that this parallelism exists between the stars in the sky and the chakras.

A portion of the human body that the Hindus have been aware of for more than 6,000 years and that is referred to as the subtle body is called the causal body. On top of this portion of the spirit, which is linked to the cosmos and serves as a support for the chakras, is the crown chakra. It is the means by which the physical body is able to concentrate on itself and by which it may connect with the energy of the cosmos. The subtle body is also known as the collective unconscious, the power of the mind to use the chakras to connect into the mind and the universe via its universal intelligence, and a condition of sleep or meditation. It is also possible to describe the subtle body as the power of the mind to use the chakras to plug into the mind and the universe.

In a manner quite similar to that of the Romans, the Hindus were aware that to be animated meant that your soul included breath. The term "prana" refers to this kind of vitality in Hinduism. People used to believe that pranatraveled through the subtle body as a stream travels through a field, carrying the energy and the liveliness from one chakra to the next in a manner that was analogous to water moving. This connection was what served to maintain the life of the person and enabled them to tap into the marvels of the cosmos that were around them. Both of these things were possible because of the person's ability to connect. People in Western cultures find it challenging to comprehend this idea since there is nothing comparable in the contemporary world that discusses the link that exists between the mind and the body. The vast majority of western religions and philosophical schools of thought focus only on the spirit, and they don't say much about the link between the two outside the fact that the body is the spirit's temple.

How to Activate Your Third Eye Chakra

Put your legs over your knees as you sit. Put your fingers together in a cross shape, with the exception of your tiny fingers, which should be brought together at the top, touched against each other, and allowed to point upward and in the opposite direction away from you. It is recommended that the right thumb be positioned on top of the left thumb. Put your attention on the crown chakra and what it stands for, which is the very top of your head.

General Principles that Will Assist You in Determining Which Chakra to Awaken

1. Get Familiar with Your Chakras

Learning about your chakras is one of the most critical steps you can take in being ready to open them. Each of the chakras has a variety of distinctive traits that are unique from those possessed by the others. That also implies that the process of opening them is rather different from other doors. When our chakras are out of balance or blocked, we may experience feelings of disorientation or exhaustion. It's possible that we'll become sick, too. Learn what each chakra stands for as well as the symptoms that indicate they are either blocked or out of balance. This will allow you to properly care for them when the situation calls for it.

The second step is to determine the extent of the need.

Because you have a total of seven chakras, also known as energy centers, you need to figure out which one you want to work on first. It is not always easy to determine which of the individuals needs assistance more than the others. This is due to the fact that any one that is out of alignment has an effect on the others. There are a few indicators that you may check up to determine which chakra is causing you the most difficulty. One of the first things you should do is do the chakra test, which is examining every region of your body to determine which one has the most issues.

In addition, you should determine whether or not you are experiencing any kind of bodily discomfort in the place that corresponds to the chakra that is being referred to. You may also evaluate what is going on in your life and discover significant concerns, such as money difficulties, safety issues, marital troubles, an emotional roller coaster, or a lack of drive, among other things. There is also the option of consulting the services of a professional who specializes in chakra energy healing, as well as a close friend or colleague who is energy-conscious.

Activate the Energy to Open Your Chakras, which Is the Third Step

You should now be able to identify the chakra that is causing you trouble. Now is the time to start making a plan for how to open that chakra, and it is essential that you also consider this to be a strategy for restoring your chakra. When you open this chakra, you are not only harmonizing the flow of your energy (both intake and outflow), but you are also expanding your awareness of the state that it may take and the ways in which it can change. The notion of balancing or achieving equilibrium while opening your chakras is the primary concept that is used by both trained healers and the majority of individuals who are energy sensitive.

During the process of opening your chakra, you will need to engage in a variety of practices, such as exercises that concentrate on your breathing and physical activities in which you direct your attention to a specific area of your body. Participate in a healing session (you may do this by finding a professional healer or an energy-conscious individual), employ chakra connection methods or massages (also known as "self-healing hands-on technique"), and practice a meditation technique that focuses on that specific chakra area.

It is important that you keep in mind that other things may present themselves throughout the process of attempting to restore your chakra using any one of these several ways. When you are working to open your chakras, it is important to keep in mind the factors that caused them to become blocked or out of balance in the first place. You should take advantage of this opportunity to proactively address these issues since they are more likely to arise in the future. Always remember to take care of yourself by making sure you are focused, attentive, and conscious of everything that is going on around you while you are opening your chakras.

When deciding which method is best for opening your chakras, it is important to first determine whatever practice most strongly speaks to you or makes the most intuitive sense. Consider whether or not you would benefit more from a contemplative or physical practice. Your availability is another factor that should be considered while selecting a practice. There's a chance you'll just have a few minutes, but there's also a chance you'll be able to book an hour or more.

A Sacral Chakra That Is Both Open And Balanced

An person who has an open sacral chakra will feel feelings, as well as have a healthy body and mind. These benefits may be attained by engaging in activities that activate the Svadhistana. Due to the fact that the individual has coped with the process of self-realization, the individual will also experience profound sentiments of joy, creativity, optimism, sexuality, and sensuality. They are unafraid to embrace themselves and have a firm grasp on their own personality, capabilities, and boundaries. This individual is able to meet their own emotional needs without the assistance of others and feels comfortable interacting with others in a variety of contexts. When your sacral chakra is in harmony, you are able to place your faith in the people around you and communicate your most private emotions. Appreciate the fact that you are able to contribute freely without anticipating receiving anything in return. The capacity to comprehend what it is that sets off our feelings and to have some degree of control over those feelings is necessary for achieving a balanced state in the sacral chakra. I can have deep and meaningful relationships. I must nurture both my body and mind. I deserve to be admired, loved, and treated kindly. These are some examples of affirmations that can inspire emotional behavior and creativity. I have control over my emotions. I cannot control the behavior of others, but I can control how I react to it. I must nurture my own creativity. I can experience pleasure by simply being myself.

A Sacral Chakra that is Working Overtime

People that are too emotional, hedonistic, and manipulative have a sacral chakra that is operating at an excessively high level. They desire to generate their own sources of pleasure, even if it is not an appropriate moment to experience any kind of pleasure at all.

Their wants take precedence above any kind of reason or regard for the welfare of other individuals. This is especially detrimental given that their needs are influencing their actions, which in turn has a negative impact on the individuals in their immediate environment.

A Sacral Chakra That Is Blocked

A person who is suffering from a blocked chakra will inevitably feel alone and lonely, and they will have a severe phobia of getting close to other people. Feelings of inadequacy and uncertainty might be brought on by having a limited sexual life and a lack of creative expression. This individual will struggle to express themselves in any form since they will keep their inhibitions to themselves and will find it difficult to do so. As time passes and the person's sacral chakra falls more out of harmony, they will acquire inclinations to be reliant on the emotional support of others, and these tendencies will become more pronounced with time. Due to the fact that the

Svadhisthanachakra is in charge of the reproductive organs, adrenal glands, and the majority of the organs located in the pelvic region, any disorders that affect any of these organs lead to a sacral chakra that is out of alignment.

The fact that it is connected to one's emotions as well as their creative potential is an intriguing aspect of this chakra. It may be found in the pelvic region, close to the area that houses the genitalia. In life, your mental state is often tied to your feelings as well as your creative output. Because of this, many people believe that the mind, and not the body, is where emotions first begin. When this chakra is blocked, it may lead to excessively outgoing conduct, such as promiscuity and living a wild lifestyle. It also refers to a lack of self-love and feelings of inadequacy, both of which may result in a person's incapacity to build intimate and meaningful relationships with other people as well as trust in them.

These Are the Seven Primary Chakras

The first, or root, chakra

Your Root chakra may be located in the base of your spine, which most people can feel in the small of their back. The color of this chakra, which is also known as the Base chakra, is a deep ruby red, very similar to the hue of a red laser light.

This chakra, which is referred to as Muladhara in Sanskrit, is responsible for keeping you rooted in the material sensations of life, survival, and instincts. It also influences fundamental feelings such as ambition, rage, and desire.

The region of the sacral chakra

Even though it is located quite near to the navel, this chakra is not often activated while one is navel gazing. You may locate it by holding two fingers below your belly button in a horizontal position. It lies tucked away at the tip of your lower finger, where it glows a vivid orange and spins like the dark core of a blazing fire or the sun at dawn and dusk.

This chakra, which influences both sexuality and creativity, is known in Sanskrit as Svadhishthana. It is essential for creative people, such as artists and other persons who express themselves sexually. Even while all of your chakras are necessary to bring your manifestations into the physical world, the sacral chakra is the primary engine that propels the majority of what you bring into existence.

Chakra of the Solar Plexus

Your solar plexus is located just below your ribcage, in the little depression that is just above your stomach. This is the natural location of your solar plexus chakra. The hue of this center is a bright and cheery yellow. In the manner of a sunflower or a gorgeous, transparent citrine gemstone.

This chakra, which is referred to as Manipura in Sanskrit, has an effect on your feeling of power as well as your self-esteem and sense of identity. Accessing your daily intuition or 'gut' feeling, as well as 'digesting' emotions and experiences, are all essential components of healthy material manifestation. The heart chakra plays an important role in all of these areas.

Your Heart chakra, which can be easily felt, is located in line with the other chakras and your actual heart. This is the region that theatrical individuals like to grasp in order to indicate how intensely they are experiencing something. The color of your Heart chakra is a rich emerald green, quite similar to the color of the "go" sign on traffic lights.

Your ability to feel and express love and compassion is impacted by your Heart chakra, which is referred to in Sanskrit as Anahata. In addition to this, it is the engine that propels your capacity to heal and connect with the planet and the creatures who surround you.

Chakra de la Throat

This chakra is located in the centre of your neck, roughly in the area where a man's Adam's apple would be. It is another chakra that is simple to locate.

The hue of it is a brilliant, transparent blue. Imagine shades of blue like sapphire and clear sky.

This blue chakra, which is associated with your capacity to communicate and tell your truth, is referred to in Sanskrit as the Vishuddha chakra.

The Chakra of the Third Eye

This well-known and shrouded energy center is located directly in the centre of your forehead. Indigo or a very dark and intense purple is the hue of it.

In Sanskrit, this faculty is referred to as Ajna, and it plays a critical role in how you see the world and the people in it. This chakra is the source of your more advanced intuition.

The top, or crown, chakra

The crown chakra is the most important one for us to focus on right now since it is situated directly above your head. You will need some time to get used to it, but you may experience it right now if you want to. For almost a half minute, rest your hand on top of your head, just above where your hair would reach. You should feel a warmth on your palm that is comparable to the warmth that comes from a candle flame. This warmth should not be felt whether you rest your hand straight on your head or if you hold your palm slightly higher. The hue of your Crown chakra may be anything from violet to white to gold, depending on your own preferences. It makes no difference whether you are unsure in the beginning. As you continue to work with your chakras, you will become more familiar with the hue associated with your Crown chakra.

Your link to the Divine, your higher intellect, and the key to a deeper awareness of who you are may all be found in the Crown chakra, which is referred to as Sahasrara in Sanskrit.

The origin and development of Chakras

If we want to know when chakras were initially acknowledged as a component of a person's ethereal and energetic body, we are going to have to go a very long way back in time. And at that point, we wouldn't have any idea what happened since nobody is aware of this information. What we do know is that an ancient Hindu document has the first known reference of chakras in the modern sense in which we define the term. That does not make the chakra system anything that is exclusive to Hinduism. Other civilizations, ranging from Japan and Korea in the east to Africa and Native American culture in the west, all have very similar notions and practices that mirror the chakra system that we'll employ today. These other cultures may be found all over the world.

The sacral energy center

The next chakra center that we will investigate is the one that is associated with our interests and gratifications. The Svadhistana Chakra, also known as the Sacral Chakra, is in charge of how you personally experience life. In the end, everything boils down to your physical sensations and the emotions you feel, and how they link you to other people. The fact that the chakra center itself is situated in the pelvic region should not come as much of a surprise given the connection that the Sacral chakra has with sexual energy. Because of this, the reproductive systems and the act of procreation in general are considered to be components of the Svadhistana. The color orange is said to be associated with this chakra point.

Your sacral chakra acts as a personal key that may be used to open doors that lead to your unique creative potential. We have already discussed how the Sacral chakra is the origin of passion, and because passion is the driving force behind creativity, it seems sense that both passion and creativity originate from the same chakra center. Despite the fact that each person's creative abilities are unique due to their beliefs, upbringing, and the society in which they are immersed, it is possible for anybody to improve their creative abilities by meditating and practicing on the chakra centers themselves. This chakra is most developed in youngsters because of their capacity to engage in play for extended periods of time, as well as their lack of inhibition when it comes to expressing their feelings and expressing themselves. Adults that resonate strongly with this chakra center are often creative types, such as painters or musicians, or they have libidos that are much higher than average. It is quite simple to overindulge in the Svadhistana, which may lead to the chakra itself being imbalanced. This is because of the nature of the chakra itself.

An imbalanced amount of sacral energy may lead to the development of unhealthy preoccupations or addictions with items that provide a heightened sense of pleasure. Sexual dysfunction and promiscuity are also quite frequent adverse effects associated with this medication. These detrimental new behaviors are likely to leave the individual feeling an overwhelming sense of guilt, which may often lead to melancholy in the affected person. Problems with the kidneys, the prostate, or the urinary and gynecological regions are some examples of the more physical elements that may become apparent. Additionally, emotional sensitivity becomes a problem, which results in a rise in the number of outbursts and fits of wrath. If one were to let things go unchecked for long enough, it's probable that they would harden their heart and lose their sensitivity, but it's not hard to stop such things from happening.

Utilizing positive affirmations that zero in on the components that are most important to balancing your Sacral chakra is the simplest approach to get started on the process. You are the only one who can make things work for you by having the belief and determination to make it happen, therefore you may either make them yourself or look for ones that already exist. The second method for stimulating this chakra center is to simply surround oneself with the color orange. This will assist. Take a bath in water that has been colored orange with food coloring for a therapy that is not only soothing but also beneficial. This works in part because of the color, and in part because water is the element that is linked with the Svadhistana chakra. In addition to being beneficial for one's general health, working out the abdominal muscles is an excellent approach to stimulate the Sacral chakra. Consuming foods with an orange tint can assist stimulate your sacral chakra as well as your sense of smell and taste since this chakra center is a sensory one. When you combine this with a few yoga positions each day, not only will you notice an increase in the flow of your energy, but you will also develop a healthier lifestyle, which will allow you to live longer and take more pleasure in the activities you most like.

Crystal Healing

Crystals and gemstones are two more tools you may use in the process of realigning and mending your chakra centers. They exude energy, which are comparable to those created by your chakras when they vibrate, due to the fact that they appear in a variety of hues and have unique forms. If they are employed, they have a tendency to realign chakras so that they return to their natural frequency of vibration, so assisting the body in its ability to cleanse itself of anything that is obstructing the flow of energy on its own.

Crystals may be used to heal, balance, and improve your chakras; a technique for doing so is outlined here.

1. Determine which crystals you will be using during the procedure, and place

them in an orderly fashion next to where you will be laying down.

2. Lie down and check to see whether you are comfortable enough, then relax and enjoy yourself.

3. To open your crown chakra, position a quartz crystal or a violet crystal right over the peak of your head and begin to focus your attention there. This encourages self-awareness and reflection.

4. Next, bring your brow chakra into alignment. Place a gemstone that is a deep shade of blue or indigo at the place just little above where your eyebrows meet.

5. To activate the fifth chakra, the throat, position a light blue crystal at the very bottom of your neck. This is done often in an effort to bring tranquility into one's life.

6. Now, go to the heart chakra of your body. Placing a green or pink crystal in the centre of your chest may help you overcome negative emotions that obstruct the flow of energy. It also encourages tranquility, which in turn boosts your overall sense of happiness.

7. When you are ready, go on to working on the chakra located in your solar plexus. By placing a yellow crystal at a spot between your ribs and navel, you may reduce feelings of worry, enhance your confidence, make your thoughts more clear, and boost your vitality.

8. To activate the sacral chakra, position an orange-colored crystal on the lower belly. This will activate the chakra. This helps in the release of tension, the balancing of creative energy, and the elimination of items in your life that get in the way of your happiness.

9. After you've finished with that, go on to focusing on your root chakra. Place a crystal of either black or red color in the space between your legs, close to the base of your spine. You also have the option of positioning two red stones of the same kind on each of your legs as an alternative. This contributes to the balance of one's bodily energies and helps one feel more grounded in reality.

You may also ground yourself by placing a stone between your feet, such as smokey quartz or black tourmaline. This stone will serve as an anchor for your energy.

The second way is to breathe.

Never underestimate the power of a good, lengthy inhale and exhale, especially if you are trying to release something from your body. The appropriate breathing methods and practices may help you release a lot from your body. It's true that breathing may cure you; in fact, it's far more potent than you would imagine.

After coming across the account of Miki Ryosuke, a Japanese actor who had back discomfort and was recommended to do some breathing methods to release the relief, he did start performing some breathing practices and was astounded by the fact that he lost weight through breathing alone. Now, his tale is quite well known, and he has developed a diet called the Miki Ryosuke's diet, which provides instructions on how to reduce body fat using breathing techniques.

I believe that every person is going to get something different from breathing practices. For example, if two people started practicing breathing, one might experience a collagen boost and wrinkles fading from his face while the other might get a childhood trauma out of his system. Breathing is not going to give everyone the same result, and I believe that every person is going to get something different from breathing practices.

Use it, think about it, and thank the god of the universe for this gift that is freely provided and that you may exercise whenever you want since it is an excellent method of letting go that doesn't cost anything. Also, don't expect for results to manifest from the very first day; give it some time since blockages don't develop overnight; it takes months, if not years, to feel and obtain the consequence of a blocked energy point, so let healing and releasing entirely to take time; dedication is really important in this process.

The concept that breath is a life-giver and that life is contained within breath itself is central to Sufism, which places a strong emphasis on the significance of breath. It is an essential instrument for healing, and when a person exudes rage and flame, the breath becomes the fire that they emit. Sufism teaches that breath is God and that God is expressed in breath, and it even indicates that the quality of one's breath is directly related to one's level of physical and mental health. A person may go for days without drinking water or eating food, but they can only go for seconds without breathing, which highlights the significance of this bodily function. The power of breath is used by the Sufi in order to connect with the supreme deity and to maintain presence in the present moment.

It is said that through breathing in this type of practice many things are manifested such as: - Slowing down the aging process, boosting the body's collagen - Creativity gets activated and IQ level is increased - Feeling cleansed and purified, free of traumas and negative energies - Feeling rejuvenated and revitalized

- Having a heightened awareness as well as enhanced senses

- A calm condition of both the mind and the body

This kind of yoga places a significant emphasis on the breath. Through proper breathing, miraculous healing may take place, and cellular renewal can take place.

"The breath travels around the body in a round, and the spine serves as the path that the breath travels along in order to complete the circle. The mystics place a tremendous deal of significance on this channel, which they refer to as the snake. The image they see in their heads is of a snake with its tail in its jaws. Almost wherever you look, you'll see a snake depicted as the conduit for the air we breathe. Kundalini is the phrase that Yogis use to refer to this energy. When this channel is made clear by the way of breathing, then this is not only helpful to the physical health, but it also opens up the powers of intuition and the doors that are inside, which is where the true happiness of man resides. When this channel is made clear by the method of breathing, then this is not only helpful to the physical health. One must adhere to the norms of mystical ablutions and rhythmic breathing in order to rid this channel of anything that stands in the way of progress. - Chapter 13, Gathas Vol.

The Heart Chakra

Green is the hue that is used to symbolize the heart chakra, and this chakra is all about maintaining good relationships, as well as love, adoration, and caring for one another. If you are able to open this specific chakra, you will find that you are more inclined to lead a joyful life. An open heart chakra will allow you to get the most out of your relationships and ensure that the people who are linked to you are content. It will also allow you to feel compassion for the people around you. To put it another way, the power of this chakra is such that it has an impact not only on you but also on the individuals in your immediate environment. You will be well loved, and the Chakra has the potential to even elevate your status among your peers.

On the other side, having a closed heart or a heart chakra that is just partially open may lead to feelings of emptiness, particularly when discussing personal connections and those with whom one is familiar. You will become hostile and resistant to attending social events if your heart chakra is closed. Because you are closed off to other people, they will respond to you with the same lack of emotion that they have towards you. After all, everything you give out will eventually come back to you.

A person who has an overactive heart chakra will have an excessive capacity for love and compassion. Because of this specific quality, the individuals around you are likely to experience feelings of suffocation and a great deal of discomfort. When you start challenging the beliefs of those closest to you and demanding answers from them, they are going to start ignoring you as a result. Despite the fact that you seem to be a lovely person, this will give the impression that you are intrusive and inquisitive. You may think that having a heart chakra that is overactive is unhealthy for long-term partnerships.

The following description is of a simple practice that may assist in opening one's heart chakra. It is important to keep in mind that for our bodies to be able to express and experience love and relationships in a way that is most conducive to human behaviors, the heart chakra must be open and functioning properly. Keeping this information in mind, you should cross your legs and sit on a surface that is level, ideally on the ground.

Put your hands on your knees, bring the very points of both of your thumbs together so that they touch the very tips of your index fingers, and then spread the rest of your fingers out in a straight line. After you have given yourself some time to relax, bring your right hand to your chest and keep it there in the same position, making sure that it is in the middle of your chest and near to your heart. You should not move your fingers and thumbs into a different position.

It is time for you to relax, and you will get there by clearing everything out of your thoughts. Consider the qualities associated with the heart chakra and the advantages it bestows. Try to picture your heart and spine in a relaxed state (without causing yourself or the procedure any stress in the process). Start reciting the "YAM" mantra as soon as you feel that you have regained your balance and calm.

If you allow your thoughts to wander and get preoccupied with things of this world, the power of this chant will not be able to work as intended. It is essential that you keep repeating the heart mantra to yourself and that you place a strong emphasis on the idea that whatever you are doing is gently and gradually making your heart cleaner. Just try to picture how calm and content you will be after you have properly opened your heart chakra.

Carry on with this exercise until you begin to feel good about yourself and until you acquire that "clean" sensation on the interior of your body.

Another item that is worth emphasizing here is something that is pretty obvious: this exercise need to be done in a quiet setting in which the possibilities of being distracted are minimized. The best time to do this is either first thing in the morning or just before you go to bed. In most cases, at this time of day, the environment around you is quiet and tranquil.

The Chakra At The Crown

Fundamentals of the Crown Chakra
The Crown chakra is the seventh and final energy center in the major chakra system. It is also the highest one. It is located at the crown of the head or just above it, and it is associated with unadulterated awareness as well as a direct link to the divine. Because this chakra is characterized as a lotus with 1,000 petals arrayed in 20 levels of 50 petals each, its Sanskrit name is Sahasrara, which means "thousand fold." This chakra is located at the crown of the head. There is a degree of overlap between this chakra and the Third Eye chakra due to the fact that the Crown chakra is also responsible for regulating the pituitary and pineal glands. In addition to this, it has control over the hypothalamus as well as the rest of the brain and skull. The color violet is the one that corresponds to it the most, however it may also be represented by a completely white hue. Ng is the

bijamantra for the Crown chakra, and it should be spoken exactly as it seems, from the very back of the throat.

A Crown Chakra that is in Good Health
When this chakra is open and operating properly, we have clear thoughts and a profound feeling of knowledge that comes from inside. We have a sense of connection to the spiritual worlds and an awareness that all things are interconnected. When the energy in our Crown chakra is under check, we are able to communicate effectively with all of creation.

Disharmonies in the Crown Chakra
When our Crown chakra is blocked, we may experience feelings of spiritual disconnection as well as cynicism. It's possible for us to feel dread of death and a sense that we aren't worthy of plenty, along with apprehension about the future and a lack of purpose. If our Crown chakra is hyperactive, we may have a tendency to be too philosophical or to have a "head in the clouds" manner

of thinking. It's possible that we would rather often be in a state of meditation than be firmly rooted in the here and now. The inability to remember things in the short term, a lack of physical coordination, and problems with the neurological system are all possible physical manifestations of an imbalance in the seventh chakra.

Minerals, Rocks, and Crystals
We may use crystals that are either clear, white, or purple in color to bring about harmony in the Crown chakra by working with these colors. Just a few examples of possible stones are amethyst, selenite, and clear or rutilated quartz. During meditation, you may either choose to hold these stones in your hands or position them straight over your head.
Bringing Back the Sense of Harmony to the Solar Plexus

Learning stimulates this chakra's energy in a positive way. As was said previously, mentally taxing yourself will provide a significant boost to the Solar Plexus chakra, which is responsible for cognition and intelligence. Even something as simple as reading a new book may be of great assistance in this regard, so there's no need to force yourself to take on something really challenging.

It doesn't even have to be a serious book; if that's where you are in life right now, a trashy romance or fantasy will do. The important thing is to add something new to what you are currently doing, and to push yourself a little bit farther than you normally would.

You may also stimulate your mind by engaging in challenging mental activities like doing puzzles, or if you're feeling really ambitious, now might be a wonderful time to enroll in a class that teaches you about a topic that you've always been curious in learning more about.

The solar plexus is connected to the sun, as one could surmise from the organ's name. Simply being exposed to sunshine may provide a considerable boost to it; thus, you should make an effort to spend time outside on bright days, or at the very least, keep yourself near windows if you are forced to remain inside.

This observation is supported by research: exposure to sunshine may help prevent depression brought on by Seasonal Affective Disorder (also known as SAD), and it can also encourage your body to create vitamin D. When we do not receive enough exposure to sunshine and vitamin D, it is common for both our energy levels and our emotions to deteriorate.

In addition to helping to restore balance to this energy, yellow beverages and foods, as well as essential oils, may be of assistance.

The chakra located in the solar plexus.

This chakra, which is located in the region of the stomach, is associated with our sense of self-worth and the value that we ascribe to ourselves. Consequently, those who struggle with low self-esteem may be experiencing an imbalance in the Solar Plexus Chakra. Because an imbalance may be the root reason of an exaggerated sense of one's own significance, people who also believe they are the focus of attention could benefit from working on this aspect of their behavior as well.

In this article, we will discuss the signs and symptoms of an imbalance in the solar plexus chakra.
Chronic weariness, liver malfunction, diabetes, high blood pressure, digestive disorders, stomach ulcers, colon illnesses, pancreatic and gallbladder troubles are all examples of physical abnormalities.

Issues pertaining to self-esteem, personal strength, and the manifestation of one's inner critic are all examples of emotional imbalances. You can feel rejected because of your physical appearance, or you might be afraid of being rejected or criticized. You may also discover that you struggle with the drive to control, rage, and ego, as well as the need to dominate others.

How to Bring Your Solar Plexus Chakra Back Into Balance

You will have healthy self-esteem, your creativity will flourish, you will be well anchored in yourself, experience self-respect and self-compassion, and be forceful, in charge, and confident when the Solar Plexus Chakra is in balance.

Practice Improving Your Breathing

Feeding your Solar Plexus Chakra may be accomplished with the use of Kapalabhati breathing or fire breathing. Because this is an advanced kind of pranayama, you need allow yourself a lot of time to become proficient at it, but the most important thing is that you should not give up.

To begin practicing fire breathing, sit down on the floor in a position that is comfortable for you. Maintaining a straight spine and pulling your neck upward can help you to stretch your core. Your neck should be long and your shoulders should be relaxed. Put your chin down and breathe vitality into your chest. Put your hands on your legs and give yourself permission to relax.

The next step is to swiftly inhale and exhale via your nose. When you are exhaling, draw your belly button in toward your spine, but when you are inhaling, relax your abdominal muscles. Because of this, air will be forced out of your nose. If you keep at it and put in the necessary effort, you'll soon have it mastered.

Exercise your ability to meditate.

Place yourself in the posture you use for meditation, still your thoughts, and then begin to imagine coals of flame emanating from the center of your navel. The following is the meditation that you should sit with: "Allow me to honor'me,' to be the person I am in the world, and to express my power and being without fear."

Accept your fear and work it into your being so that it becomes a part of you. You are not rejecting your fear when you decide to become conscious of your own strength; rather, you are acknowledging that you are afraid and then deciding to go with whatever it is that you are afraid of doing nonetheless.

Acoustic Medicine

The Solar Plexus Chakra, also known as the manipura, vibrates to the note "E." Chanting RA in the key of "E" can assist in bringing the chakra back into alignment!

Imagine the color yellow in your mind.

Yellow is the color that represents the Solar Plexus Chakra in the human body. Imagine a stunning sunflower or dahlia blooming close to your solar plexus chakra. They are both bright yellow and huge. You could also use candles that are yellow, or you could surround yourself with photographs of things that are yellow. When this starts to take place, you will become aware of a warm glow emanating from the Manipura.

The sacral energy center

This Chakra is all about pleasure, satisfaction, and even sexuality and a feeling of abundance despite its location in the bottom area of the belly. It is also known as the sacral chakra. Because of this, it is considered to be a particularly sensitive chakra, and an imbalance in this chakra may lead to emotions of disappointment and even a lack of desire to engage in sexual activity.

The Third Eye, Also Known As The Brow Chakra

This is the fifth chakra, and it is placed in the middle of the forehead. It resonates with the color pink, and it is associated with a heavenly insight, an inner vision, intellect, and wisdom. Intuition is also associated with this chakra. Our capacity to concentrate on the bigger picture and our level of awareness are inextricably linked to one another. It is represented as a descending triangle inside a circle, and the diamond is its precious stone. This chakra is personified by the sun, and the spiral that corresponds to it is known as the sacral chakra. It is represented by the sixth sense in our language.

If you are able to picture things via your third eye and have a high degree of intuition as well as a direct spiritual vision, this indicates that your third eye chakra is open and functioning properly. When your third eye chakra isn't functioning properly, you become dogmatic in your thinking and too dependent on the truth of your views. You may have a propensity to put your trust in those in authority, and you may not be very adept at thinking on your own. An overactive third eye chakra may cause a person to live in a dream world and may even cause hallucinations to occur.

Eyestrain, headaches, blindness, and impaired vision are some of the physical symptoms that may occur when there are issues with the third eye chakra. The eyes, face, brain, and lymphatic and endocrine systems are the elements of the body that are related with the brow, often known as the third eye. In general, the third eye chakra is where greater intuition, the energies of the spirit and light, and psychic abilities are centered. This is the reason why the third eye chakra is associated with the element of light. With the help of its abilities, the system rids you of negativity as well as inclinations toward self-centeredness, provides advice, and connects you with your higher self.

Visualization for Healing of the Third Eye Chakra

Since our third eye serves as the starting point for all of our dreams and visions, visualizations are the most effective technique. Our perceptions are twisted and reshaped in the third eye. Through the use of this method, the third eye may be properly repaired.

Consume meals that range from red to purple in hue.

Consuming foods with a purple hue, such as purple potatoes, blackberries, plums, and purple grapes, is an effective way to promote the healing of your third eye chakra. Your brow chakra may also be healed with the consumption of chocolate and spices or drinks scented with lavender.

Yoga Perform child positions as well as other postures that include forward bends in your yoga practice. Performing eye exercises is another fantastic method for enhancing the energy of your third eye chakra. After doing these exercises, you may find that applying a soothing herbal oil helps.

Bringing Our Life Force Into Harmony And Purification

The throat chakra, also known as the Vishuddhi chakra, is located close to the larynx. It is the center that assists us in cleansing not just our bodies but also our thoughts and feelings. The poisons that build up in our bodies are flushed out via our throat chakra, which helps to maintain our overall health. Our capacity to 'think before speaking' is improved, and we acquire the ability to communicate more clearly as a result. We hone the nuanced skill of using words tactfully in order to protect the feelings of others.

One of the most admirable qualities of human beings is their capacity for introspection. The practice of meditation gives us the opportunity to reflect on our actions of the past and prompts us to question the caliber of our ideas, behaviors, and feelings. On the one hand, we want for love and relationships that are honest and open with one another.

On the other hand, our anxieties and complexes are a constant presence in our lives and hinder us from being honest with ourselves.

We have come to the conclusion that we are the sum total of our positive and negative ideas, feelings, and actions. In the same way that we have been harmed by the malicious words said by other people, we have also been victims of our own wrath and grief, and we have taken it out on other people. We are aware that, in some way, shape, or form, we contributed in some way to the issue at hand, and we know that placing blame on others will not relieve us of the burden of guilt that accompanies us.

Nevertheless, the core of each positive and negative experience propels us forward along the road of spiritual, emotional, and mental development. Each new adventure forces us to expand our horizons and brings us closer to adulthood. We are able to learn to center our attention on the genuine significance of our life so that we are not swept away by the sway of our ideas and feelings. We are aware that we have been given a tremendous amount of potential blessings. All that is required of us is to tap into it and channel it so that we may live lives that have greater significance.

We will, for the first time, start to accept the truth about ourselves, which is that we were the obstacles in the way of our own advancement on the road toward improvement. We cultivate the virtue of patience and begin to direct our attention on developing our own unique skills and capabilities. This chakra is associated with artistic endeavors that are in some way linked to the vocal chords, such as teaching, writing, singing, and composing poetry.

Practices That Are Useful Sitting in silence for a period of time on a regular basis is a very straightforward and efficient method that trains us to think before we speak. We acquire the ability to choose our words carefully.

We are more able to connect with our authentic selves when we chant the mantra HAM. This mantra guides us through the process of being more self-aware and assists us in developing our full potential.

Pranayama, often known as breathing exercises, are the most effective approach to cleanse and balance this chakra.

This chakra is represented by the color blue, which is also its related color. This chakra may be activated, cleansed, and calmed with the use of crystals like as aquamarine, apatite, turquoise, and blue tiger eye.

In the course of our meditation sessions, we gain clarity as we concentrate on the part that we play in each circumstance. It's possible that we've caused harm to other people without even recognizing it, and what's more significant is that we could have caused harm to ourselves by burying the anguish and suffering that was created by other people. We are taught to communicate in a kind and diplomatic manner. The other person is given the ability to think independently as a result of this empowerment. We acquire the ability to articulate our perspectives, feelings, and ideas in a straightforward and uncomplicated manner.

The jalandharibandha, ujjayipranayam, matsyasana, sarvangasana, and shirsasana, setuasana, and other yoga postures are some of the breathing and stretching activities that are associated with the throat chakra.

The Process Of Cleaning Your Chakras

When you have mastered opening and shutting your Chakras, the next step is to clean them, which is an easy step to do. It will take some time before you are able to identify where there are roadblocks; but, if you practice regularly, you will become pretty competent at this rather soon.

Your energy flow will become slow if one or more of your chakras is blocked, even if it's just partially obstructed. You need to train yourself to differentiate between energy that is freely moving through a Chakra point and energy that is having difficulty doing so.

Clearing the obstructions that have accumulated through time is a necessary step in the process of cleansing your Chakras. Because you will have a lifetime's worth of accumulation, the first time you do this, it may take two or three efforts to totally remove them, but you will feel the difference simply by clearing a little number of them.

The process of eliminating obstructions in a pipe is quite similar to the process of clearing blockages in your energy points. When employing a pipe, fluid is sent down the pipe at a high pressure in order to dislodge whatever is causing it to get clogged. The method is the same with each of your Chakras. The key distinction is that, rather than water, you boost the velocity and pressure of the flow of energy. When the obstacle is overcome, the blocked energy is released into the flowing energy field surrounding you, where it is then dispersed.

As you get further up, you will need to apply a greater amount of pressure since the obstructions from the lower Chakras are building up. When you initially begin to do this, I would suggest that you slow down a little and concentrate on opening one chakra at a time before moving on to the next. Begin with the Crown Chakra and clear out any obstructions you find there.

When you have finished clearing the Crown Chakra, descend down to the Third Eye Chakra and begin working to free up the obstruction there. Continue with this by pulling it up from the Third Eye into the Crown, and then outward from there.

Carry on in this manner, taking each Chakra in turn and passing it through the transparent Chakras that are located above it. This takes longer, but since you will definitely have a great deal of build-up, it will be more successful than starting from the beginning and attempting to force it all through in one go.

After you have performed an initial cleaning, you may then proceed to do a cleansing that works its way from the ground up. It is highly recommended that you do this activity on a consistent basis and at least once a month.

After you have done cleaning, it is imperative that you do not forget to seal the Chakras and reduce the flow of energy to a trickle.

Chakras are energy points that may be located along the central meridian of our bodies, to give them their most basic description. The ancient Sanskrit name for it translates to "circle" or "wheel." According to historical accounts, the concept of chakras originated in the Vedas, which are known to be part of the Hindu texts. Acupuncture is only one of many traditions that makes reference to chakras. Other traditions do as well.

There are seven primary chakras in the body. In addition, the following are included on the list:

The first, or root, chakra

This area of the body, which is positioned between the anus and the genitals, is referred to as the root chakra. It is a symbol of one's connection to the Earth or of their groundedness. It is connected to a feeling of foundation as well as a sense of security. It is thought that the root chakra is the location of new beginnings and untapped potential.

The sacral energy center

The region of the groin contains the location of the second chakra. The sacral chakra is related with relationship in all of its forms, including romantic and platonic partnerships. It has been linked to sexuality as well as the creative process. This chakra is associated with our relationships with other people. In addition to this, it is responsible for our capacity to welcome new experiences as well as the involvement of other people in our life.

The chakra located in the solar plexus.

This chakra may be found in the region of the stomach, more specifically in the area of the upper abdomen. It is related to self-confidence, self-esteem, and feeling that one's own worth something. It has something to do with the degree to which we are able to direct our own lives. In its most basic sense, the third chakra is where our will is centered.

The Chakra of the Heart

The location of the heart is suggested by the name of the fourth chakra, which is located there. It has something to do with our capacity to love. Unconditional love is something that is encouraged by the heart chakra. This entails having an unconditional love for oneself in addition to having an unconditional love for other people. It is connected to feelings of love, happiness, and inner tranquility.

This is the Throat Chakra.

This chakra may be found in the area of the neck. It has something to do with one's voice and one's ability to communicate. Although the throat chakra is not only related with the act of expressing oneself, this is how we convey our thoughts, ideas, and concepts to others. Most significantly, this chakra urges us to voice our own particular truths and to do it in a loving manner.

The Chakra of the Forehead

The area in between the eyes on the forehead is home to the third eye chakra, which is another name for the forehead chakra. It shows our capacity to focus or concentrate as well as our awareness of the bigger picture. It is connected to one's imagination as well as their intuition. Additionally, the frontal chakra is associated with intelligence, as well as our capacity to discriminate and make choices.

The third eye chakra is in charge of cleansing ourselves of any bad inclinations that we may have. In addition to this, it helps us get rid of self-centeredmindsets. We are able to get direction by using the energy that comes from our forehead chakra. In addition to this, it helps us to connect with or channel our Higher Selves.

The sixth chakra is intimately connected to one's capacity for visual perception. It is connected with a variety of different kinds of psychic talents, one of which being clairvoyance.

The Chakra at the Crown

The crown chakra may be located at the very top of our heads. It is a representation of our relationship with the skies and with awareness. The spiritual realm is represented by the crown chakra.

It is the center of everything that is enlightening, energetic, and thought-provoking. It promotes an increase in the outward flow of knowledge. The gift of cosmic awareness is one of the unique benefits that come to us as a result of the development of the crown chakra.

We are able to reach both the unconscious as well as the subconscious when there is balance and a healthy flow of energy in this chakra. It paves the way for us to particularly open ourselves up to the Divine. On the other side, an imbalance in the crown chakra may lead to emotions of irritation and other forms of negative emotion. It has the potential to deprive us of delight.

The Importance of the Seven Chakras

It is essential for the alignment and balance of all aspects of our physical bodies, including hormones, chemicals, and other bodily functions. We will be able to have healthy lives and experience increased vitality if we do this. In a similar manner, in order to establish a healthy chakra energy system, all seven of the primary chakras need to be in balance.

Our chakra system has repercussions for more than just our bodily well-being. It has a significant bearing on not only our mental but also our emotional and spiritual well-being as well.

Certain aspects of the body are associated with each chakra. Therefore, if even one of the chakras is out of alignment, the whole system will be thrown off. Additionally, our health is in jeopardy because of this.

When you practice working on your chakras, you also help your body heal. And this is the secret to living a life that is not just healthy but also pleasant, gratifying, and balanced.

Mindful breathing is covered in Chapter 3, which focuses on Manipura, the Solar Plexus. Consider how having this level of command over your breathing affects your state of mind.

The Chakra of Self-Control

The ManiPura, or Solar Plexus, is the third energy node in our body and is positioned only a few inches above the navel. It is also more popularly known as the Sacral Plexus. This Chakra is related to our emotional lives, but it also controls how we see ourselves, which is possibly a more significant function. It controls our levels of self-esteem and self-confidence, as well as how we understand our own sense of value. Therefore, as you should hopefully be starting to understand, the Solar Plexus deals primarily and in part with our sense of vision, as well as our personal strength and our ability to exert control.

A significant number of persons who have adopted the concept of chakras believe that successful people—those who thrive in their occupations, have discovered pleasure via their own means, or are financially independent—have a particularly active Solar Plexus. It is undeniably a thought-provoking proposition. After fact, the majority of successful people do have high self-esteems, approach challenging circumstances with confidence, and have a strong sense of their own sense of worth.

Activate Your Solar Plexus Chakra

When the energy in our Solar Plexus is under check, we are able to flourish. We face difficult circumstances with a special clarity, we solve problems in an effective manner, and we have faith in our own ability to choose the best course of action. Confidence and a sense of self-worth, on the other hand, might briefly vanish along with the Solar Plexus when it becomes imbalanced.

Signs and Symptoms of a Solar Plexus Chakra That Is Closed

Disorganized thinking

Depressive state

Dominance is the outcome of having a Solar Plexus that is overactive.

The dread of being rejected

Lack of capacity to make choices or judgments.

a deficit in one or more of the following: self-esteem; self-confidence; and/or self-worth

Passivity is the outcome of a Solar Plexus that is not functioning properly.

Foods That Help Open the Solar Plexus

foods that are yellow in hue, such as maize and cornmeal

Oatmeal and granola are examples of grains.

Whole grain bread and raisins are both good sources of fiber.

Tea made with chamomile

Exercises That Help Open the Solar Plexus

Stepping out: Dancing needs a certain amount of self-control since we need to regulate how our feet move to the rhythm of the music, how our legs carry us across the dance floor, and how our arms move so that they are not just hanging limp at our sides. Dancing demands exactly the perfect amount of physical control to throw open our Solar Plexus or bring it back to the state of equilibrium it was in when we were first born. It doesn't really matter what kind of dance you perform; as long as you're moving and maintaining control of your body, dancing is a practice that tends to be quite beneficial.

The "Boat Pose" is another exercise that requires us to have total control of our bodies and is an excellent remedy for anybody who may have an imbalance in their Solar Plexus. You should proceed in the following manner:

1. Before beginning this exercise, choose an area on the floor that is level, firm, and supporting all at the same time.

2. While keeping your bottom firmly planted on the floor, progressively rise the upper and lower parts of your body until they create the shape of a V. 3. Hold this position for as long as you feel comfortable.

3. Extend both of your arms so that they are perpendicular to the ground in front of you. Allow the inside of each extended

arm to softly press on the outside of each of the thighs. Do not support your body or your legs by using your arms to hold them up.

4. Maintain this posture for the next thirty seconds. Focus your attention on the way you are breathing.

5. After the first thirty seconds, drop both your upper and lower halves back to the floor in a gradual and controlled manner. After you have rested for one minute, repeat the exercise another two more times, bringing the total number of repetitions to three.

"I am able to articulate my thoughts in a manner that is graceful and honest."

My throat chakra has always been the one that has been the most challenging for me to maintain open. It is imperative that I continue to work on it so that it does not become unusable again. In my family, thyroid problems run rampant, and I've struggled mightily with a number of neck issues over the years. However, this only addresses the purely physical aspects of the Throat chakra. There is also an emotional component, which consists of learning how to advocate for oneself and learning how to take ownership of one's own authenticity. You may shut this down by listening to the pessimistic discourse of everyone else. If this is the case, you are the one who is engaging in negative self-talk. Your Throat chakra will begin to constrict if you do not make an effort to articulate what is true to you. If your Throat chakra is blocked, it will be extremely difficult for you to interact with other people. When my throat chakra is entirely blocked, I find it far easier to isolate myself in the midst of a thick forest or up in the mountains than to engage in conversation with even a single person. If you are sick with a cold, a sore throat, or a sinus infection, give some thought to the truth that lies inside you.

It may be quite draining on the Throat chakra for persons whose jobs need them to engage with the general public on a regular basis. It is possible that your Throat chakra may shut up on you despite your best efforts to prevent it from happening no matter how hard you try to keep it open. After then, the only thing you can do is continue to work on unlocking it from that point on. Having a sore throat is often a warning indication that you are bottling up your feelings or failing to express yourself. This is due to an accumulation of bad energy that has been stuck in your Throat chakra.

Activating your Throat chakra may be accomplished most effectively by letting your soul be heard. This may be done in whatever manner of expression with which you are most at ease. Even while verbal exchange is the most effective method of communication, this is not always about words. Singing, drawing, typing, or any other method of expression that comes to mind are all forms of communication. This might even be documented in a personal diary. Communicate, communicate, and communicate some more!!!!!!!! Release whatever you've been harboring inside of you for so long. Give vent to the feelings that you have repressed for so long inside of you. Keep a diary if you are confident in your writing abilities so that you may record the thoughts and feelings that you are unable or unable to share with the rest of the world. You will be able to repair and unleash the potential of your Throat chakra so long as you release it and do not cling to it in any way. Crystals are also of great assistance in working with the Throat chakra. You may choose any or all of the crystals that are associated with the Throat chakra to make a necklace for yourself.

Producing any kind of music or noise might also be of assistance. It is not even necessary for them to be words. whatever it is that makes you feel the most at ease.

Treatment With Reiki Is Effective For A Variety Of Illnesses

Please take notice that each of the solutions that are provided below also includes the sort of hand postures that you may use in order to accomplish the outcomes that you are looking for. It is not enough to just place one's hands on another person's body; one must also convey the energy of the universe. The practitioner will proceed in the same manner even if you are the receiver.

Now, the reason why the majority of illnesses are mentioned together in one section is because the essential hand positions for the Reiki therapy are comparable to those of the ailments themselves.

Pain in the Head and Back both

When it comes to headaches, there is no one posture that applies to everyone at the same time; thus, you may test everything and then settle on whichever one is the most helpful.

The Leading Position

The first thing you need to do is move your hand in a parallel direction from the top of the head to the area of the upper teeth, and then move it to the right and left sides of the nose. This will be the beginning of the evaluation.

Coming in at number two

The hands of the practitioner should be cupped around the back of the recipient's head, and the practitioner's fingers should be placed on the medulla oblongata. This is the soft region that runs down the midline of the head to the neck and is halfway to where the hard bone transitions into a soft depression. It is also halfway to where the hard bone terminates.

The hands of the healer should be positioned in the third position, which is between the shoulder blades and the shoulders of the patient.

Fourth Position At this stage, you should keep your hands resting on top of your shoulder blades.

The hands should next be placed on the bottoms of the feet, which is the fifth position. More specifically, the tips of the big toes need to be protected by the covering.

Ailment of the back

In addition to the hand Reiki postures described below, you may also try some local backache therapy.

The first position requires the practitioner to put his or her hands in a parallel posture from the area of the upper teeth to the forehead, and then to the right and left sides of the nose.

Second Position At this point, your hands should be resting on top of your shoulders and across your shoulder blades.

Third Position Bring the palms of the hands together and place them on top of the shoulder blades.

Place in Order Four

The hollows of the knees should be covered by the palms of the hands.

Placed in Fifth Position

The hands should then be placed on the recipient's foot soles in this position. More specifically, the tips of the big toes need to be protected by the covering.

Chakra Guide

The following is an explanation of all of the primary chakras of the body, along with the characteristics that are often connected with each one. You may also utilize this list to assist you in diagnosing any specific issues that you may be having with a certain chakra imbalance that you may be experiencing.

1. The first chakra, or the root.

The chakra is situated underneath the body and the spine, namely in the region around the tailbone and the base of the spine. Symbolizes both our sense of being grounded and our basis in this world.concerns with safety, fundamental requirements for existence, and the ability to continue existing.

2. The Sacral Chakra is situated in the region of the lower belly, about two to

three inches below the navel. Symbolizes our connection to other people as well as our openness to trying new things, taking joy in things, and experiencing a sense of fulfillment.

3. The Solar Plexus Chakra is situated in the middle of the belly, directly below the rib cage. Symbolizes the sense of affluence and self-assurance that we have.

4. The Heart Chakra The heart chakra is located in the middle of our chest, just over our heart, and it is the hub of our emotions related to love, joy, and serenity.

5. Throat Chakra The Throat Chakra is located in the middle of the throat and is symbolic of our capacity to communicate with others, our self-expression, our confidence, and our understanding of the truth.

6. The Third Eye Chakra The third eye chakra is situated in the middle of the forehead, between the eyes. It is symbolic of our intuition, imagination, knowledge, and capacity to think and make judgments.

7. The third eye chakra

The crown chakra is the most powerful chakra in the body, and its location is at the topmost pinnacle of the head, just above the vertical line of the spine. It is a representation of our connection to the spiritual realm, as well as knowledge and happiness.

Contribute to the Regeneration of the Chakras of Others!

Not only can you use color therapy to rebalance and strengthen your own chakras, but you can also use it to assist improve the chakras of your family members, loved ones, and friends. When you see a member of your immediate or extended family going through a challenging period in their life, you may lend them a hand by making use of this resource. This kind of healing is known as "Distant Healing."

Exercise in Long-Distance Healing:

When doing distance healing, envision the individual (visualize them in your mind -- or third eye) and send them the white light that was described before in the exercise for the crown chakra. Now, visualize this white light beginning at their feet and moving upward while round their body three times. The motion should be clockwise. The next step is to see the various hues of light associated with each chakra moving in a spiral around the person's chakras and then moving downward and upward along their body.

I have personally done this for members of my own family, loved ones, and friends, and they have all informed me that they felt more tranquil, joyful, and in charge of their life, as well as that they were better able to deal and cope with the circumstances that they were now in. You won't be able to deny the efficacy of ColorTherapy after you've seen it for yourself; you will definitely notice a change!

The methods of chakra-balancing color therapy are very efficient and result-oriented, so they may help you enhance all elements of your health, including the physical, mental, and spiritual components. You will eventually be able to go about your daily life with a beautifully soothing feeling of inner peace, stability, and happiness. This will allow you to live your life to the fullest. The fact that these procedures for balancing the chakras are offered without charge is another wonderful aspect of them. It is a free global gift that just needs you and your mind (or third eye), therefore there is no reason to believe that this is a business-formed hoax that promises it can sell happiness to you. So do yourself a favor and start seeing the colors around you!

The Qualities That Are Associated With Each Chakra

Every chakra has one-of-a-kind qualities and serves a particular purpose; the degree to which these qualities and functions are expressed depends on the state of the chakra. The chakras are responsible for distributing energy to various regions of the body, and they also have a connection to the frequency of the vibrations. The state of a chakra's health may be determined by whether or not it is open or active and whether or not energy flows easily through it. It is an indication that there is an issue someplace if the chakra is blocked, congested, sluggish, dark, or even overstimulated.

There is a close connection between our physical, mental, and emotional bodies, as well as all of the subtle bodies, and the chakras. Because there are so many of them, and because scientists are always finding new ones via their study, compiling a list of all of their characteristics would be very challenging. The following is a list of the most important characteristics and terms that will assist you in getting started with your chakra exploration.

CROWN CHAKRA is the seventh chakra.

The connection to the unseen realm is made via the crown chakra. When a chakra is functioning properly, it acts as a conduit via which information may be received from the unseen world, and it also allows the light of the cosmos to enter the body. This light represents unadulterated love.

On the other hand, when our chakra is blocked or closed, it is often because of the training that we have received from our society, which prohibits us from believing anything other than what can be shown by science or through real and actual proof. When people are born, they virtually always have closed minds and disconnected minds. Because of this, when our crown is closed, it is more challenging to think, and particularly to experience, that we are one with life. We have a sense of being separated from one another, and we are brimming with the worries and illusions that are conditions of the society of "subway, work, sleep," as well as an education that is too rigorous and too distant from the reality.

The Chakra of the Third Eye is the Sixth Chakra.

The third eye chakra is associated to the neurological system, as well as the eyes and the nose. Both hemispheres of the brain are given a boost as a result. It has an effect on any and all organs that are associated to the third eye. When the third eye chakra is out of alignment, it may cause problems with the eyes, sinuses, head (fog or mental weariness), difficulties being positive, as well as learning and attention disorders. These issues can also make it difficult to remain optimistic.

Because the sixth chakra awakens our inner senses, it paves the way for us to achieve more consciousness as well as greater access to the truth and to things that cannot be seen. It is not the sole chakra that is responsible for our intuition, but it plays a significant part in the process. It is said that activating the third eye also stimulates all of the other chakras in the body. The third eye is said to trigger extra-perception. When our third eye is open and functioning properly, we experience increased intuition, imagination, creativity, and clarity, as well as increased vitality.

Meditations With Chakra Mantras To Release Pent-Up Energy

Vibrations are what make up sound. What you may not be aware of is that each of your chakras also has a distinct frequency. You may employ mantras that are known to be in vibrational harmony with each chakra, with the goals of opening and balancing the system via the use of mantras that are known to be in vibrational harmony with each chakra.

During meditation, reciting chakra mantras may have a very significant influence on the practitioner. Imagine a mantra to be a tuning fork, and a chakra to be a utensil. When you strike the tuning fork, the utensil will come into vibrational resonance with the tuning fork, releasing any blocked energies that do not share the same resonance.

Mantras of the Five Seeds

Let's start with some fundamental chants known as bija mantras, also known as seed mantras, which have been utilized all around the world in various forms of meditation to bring one's energy into balance.

"Aum" is the correct pronunciation of OM. The one of the bija mantras that is the most well recognized and used today. It is the sound of creation, also known as the anahatnaad, and it causes energy to accumulate and flow upward into the crown chakra and then forth into the cosmos. The mantra that represents acceptance and agreement is OM. It enables us to embrace our more evolved selves and clears the way for open and unrestricted energy flow throughout. In addition to this, it functions as a collecting mantra, allowing you to concentrate on gathering your inside energy and getting your energy ready for action.

KRIM (pronunciation: "kreem") is a mantra that, when chanted, causes our lower chakras to become active and begin the process of cleaning our body by elevating its vibrations.

SHRIM (should be pronounced "shreem"): It is related to the head and the third eye in some way. However, it may also be employed to bring beauty to one's existence and enjoyment to one's senses in addition to fostering physical and spiritual enlightenment.

The name HRIM (pronounced "hreem") refers to the abilities of creativity and healing that it has. The recitation of this mantra cleanses the heart and brings about an awakening of compassion.

HUM (pronounced "hoom"): This causes a breakdown in negative sentiments and promotes optimism and vigorthroughout the body. It is pronounced as "hoom."

After reading the list, choose the mantra (or mantras) that you feel drawn to follow based on your gut instincts. There are seven chakras in your body, and each of the cleaning mantras relates to one of those chakras. You may be highly "energetically healthy" in certain regards, but not so much in others, so you shouldn't worry about employing all of them.

Simply choose the one that speaks to your requirements (you can ask yourself, "Does this sound helpful to me?"), and then use it as a springboard to begin your meditation practice. This figuratively "settles the score" for your meditation, after which you are ready to bring in the curative energies of the purifying mantras that have been discussed here.

The Chakras, Counted to Seven

There are hundreds of points in your body at which energy may be directed and concentrated. Chakras, on the other hand, are the names given to the seven primary locations at which the primary energy centers are situated. Every portion of your body is adequately represented along the chakra route, which runs from the base of your spine to the crown of your head. The seven chakras in your body are distributed between these two points. The chakras are responsible for the flow of energy from the crown of the head all the way down to the base of the spine. Each chakra in your body relates to a different facet of your awareness and performs a unique set of tasks.

In addition, each chakra has a particular gland within the endocrine system of the body that it is associated with, as well as a hue that falls somewhere on the spectrum of the rainbow. On some level—emotional, mental, physical, or spiritual—the knowledge contained in each hue may be accessed. This knowledge is often used in the process of chakra healing and balancing via the utilization of a technique known as color healing; we will discuss this later on in the lesson.

An illustration of the seven primary chakras and their associated auric fields may be seen below.

1. The Chakra of the Root (Base)

This energy point, known as the chakra, is the first of the seven. It may be found near the bottom of the spine, just slightly above the genital region, and the color red that corresponds to it in the rainbow spectrum describes its appearance. The base of the spine, the feet, the rectum, the legs, the bones, the sexual organs, the immune system, the pelvis, the appendix, the bladder, and the hips are all related with the root chakra. Additionally, it is connected to the concepts of anchoring, rooted, and support.

Additionally, the link between your former incarnations and the ground, as well as your levels of physical vitality and your desire to exist in the physical world, are all aspects that are related with the root chakra. Before your energy may access the higher chakra centers, it must first be transmuted and refined by this chakra. This is the primary function of this chakra.

This chakra is where sexually inspired energy is generally held, and you can always activate it via yoga to cause it to ascend through each of the other chakras and all the way up to the crown chakra. Your awareness and the spiritual development of other levels of energy will increase as you continue to do this.

You'll have a strong desire to life, and you'll be brimming with physical vitality, if you keep your root chakra open and make sure it's functioning properly. Your physical vitality is cut off when it is weak or obstructed, and you are unable to make a powerful physical impression when this occurs.

In the event that your root chakra is underdeveloped, you will experience a loss of both physical strength and coordination. You will notice that you avoid engaging in any kind of physical activity, and it will be difficult for you to physically express yourself. If your root chakra is weak, you may also get the sensation of not being grounded and of lacking a solid basis.

If it reaches to the point where it is too reactive, you will never be able to be happy with simply being in one location, and you will be seeking for something to do or someplace to go all the time. If your root chakra is open but not working properly, you may have a predisposition toward aggressive behavior in the physical world.

This chakra is related with a number of different bodily ailments, such as persistent lower back pain, stress in the spine, constipation, pelvic discomfort, sexual potency issues, urinary difficulties, colon cancer, and so on. Insecurities, aggressive behavior, gluttony, and resentment are some of the other issues that are linked to the root chakra.

2. The Sacral Chakra, located in the lower abdomen

The orange hue in the rainbow spectrum corresponds to the sacral chakra, which may be found around one to two inches below your naval and is positioned in the lower part of your body. Ovaries, testicles, genital organs, the womb, kidneys, pancreas, and adrenal glands are all connected to this condition. The sacral chakra is the location where sexual energy, unfiltered emotions, and creative expression are focused.

This chakra absorbs oxygen directly from the air, turns it into energy, and then uses that energy to facilitate spiritual awareness, sexuality, integration, and creative expression. In addition to this, it is founded on the concepts of power and raw energy, and it is related with water.

You will typically have a great deal of sexual energy, power, and healing energy while it is open. In addition to this, you have a high degree of creative ability and focus mostly on artistic pursuits. However, if the chakra located in your lower belly is blocked, your sexual experience will be weak, you will feel dissatisfied, and at times you may suffer from poor self worth. This is because your sexual energy will be unable to flow freely.

It's possible that your second chakra is out of whack if you struggle with feelings of guilt. If it is out of balance, you are also likely to have difficulties with money, in which you feel unworthy of spending money on yourself. If it is out of balance, it is probable that you will have both of these problems. On the other side, if this chakra is hyperactive, the effect may be uncontrolled sexual energy with a lot of concentration on material things. This is because this chakra is located in the sacral region of the body. Other bad consequences of the lower abdominal chakra include sexual problems, the desire to possess, overindulging in food, jealously, envy, and perplexity. Other negative aspects of the lower abdomen chakra include.

When it is in a state of harmony, this chakra is related with positive characteristics as well. A few excellent examples are working well with people, having tolerance, being open to new ideas, giving and receiving love passionately, and giving and getting gifts.

3. The Chakra of the Solar Plexus

This chakra may be found at the middle of the body, just below the sternum and directly above the navel. In the range of colors that make up the rainbow, it is denoted by the yellow hue. It is connected to the gastrointestinal tract, the liver, the pancreas, and the neurological system, as well as the muscles. Because it is connected to things like your own willpower, integrity, intention, and metabolic energy, it plays a very significant part in the functioning of your body.

Your urges and impulses are brought to you via the solar plexus chakra, and your emotions are under its control. It is also connected to the element of fire, and it serves as the basis of your personality. As the basis of your personality, it determines your responses and the emotions that you experience, such as happiness or despair.

When the solar plexus chakra is open and balanced, it brings with it a feeling of wellbeing, tranquility, and tenderness, as well as a tremendous emotional power. When everything is in check, it bolsters your strength by providing you with personal inspiration. When it is out of whack, it has the potential to generate undesirable ideas and behaviours. If this pathway is blocked, it may also contribute to panic episodes. You can have a persistent feeling of insecurity and weakness and be easily bullied into not making your own choices.

Pancreatitis, adrenal issues, hepatitis, intestinal disorders, duodenal ulcers, diabetes, liver malfunction, and arthritis are some of the medical ailments that are connected with this chakra.

Trust, fear, self-confidence, self-care, intimidation, responsibilities in decision making, sensitive to personal honor and self esteem are some of the emotional and spiritual concerns associated with the solar plexus chakra. The qualities associated with this chakra include authority, self control, mastery of desire, personal power, immortality, humor, laughter, and radiance.

4. The Chakra of the Heart

The location of the heart chakra is in the middle of the chest, about two to three inches higher than the solar plexus. In the range of colors that make up the rainbow, it is denoted by the color green. The heart, the glands, the arms, the circulatory system, the lungs, the breast, the ribs, and the diaphragm are the bodily organs that are connected with this chakra.

The love and compassion that are at the core of our being are housed in the heart chakra. In addition to this, it is associated with feelings such as contentment, reverence, honesty, generosity, and pleasure. This is the reason why in many cultures, the heart is said to be the mother of all of us and the seat of the soul. Additionally, the sensation of connection with other people is brought about through the heart chakra.

When the heart chakra is activated, it serves as a conduit for the flow of unconditional love, and the qualities associated with having a good heart are distributed throughout the whole body. In addition to this, it replaces your anxieties with compassion in the form of spiritual love, which is an essential instrument that brings about wholeness. In addition to this, it plays a significant part in the spiritual healing process.

On the other side, if your heart chakra is blocked, you will feel an inadequate flow of emotional sustenance and love. As a result, you will be more likely to experience unpleasant emotions such as egotism, impatience, guilt, hate, and a variety of other feelings.

Because your heart chakra is blocked, you won't be able to experience love for other people, and your relationship with yourself will become unhealthy and narcissistic. It is possible that you will spend your whole life carrying a great deal of stress in each and every region of your body. The bitterness and rage that are stuffed deep inside your heart will, in due time, accumulate to the point where they will emerge as an illness.

5. The Chakra of the Throat

This is the mother chakra, and it is associated with creative expression, expressing oneself authentically, and even communication. The throat chakra is responsible for the control of one's ability to communicate verbally. This chakra is associated with clairaudience, which refers to one's capacity to pick up on the tones and vibrations of spiritual communication, as well as with the element of sound. This chakra is also involved with the process of reception, which might include things like music, language, sounds, scents, and taste.

The solar plexus sends ideas to the throat chakra, commonly known as our voice, and the throat chakra relays those thoughts in a manner that is more tangible. The body's throat chakra is activated to produce feelings of love, joy, and serenity when it is working in conjunction with the heart chakra.

In most cases, our life experiences are immediately translated into our ideas, after which they are changed into words, and finally, they are translated into deeds with the assistance of this chakra, which directs and focuses our thoughts into language. The tremendous power that our voice possesses has the capacity to change our desires and intentions, and even to help us bring our dreams to life.

When the throat chakra is opened, the divine will is brought into harmony, which results in a deep awareness of the purpose of life and the cosmos as well as a feeling of liberation.

The opening of this chakra, together with the proper functioning of sound, makes it possible to embrace others with love and warmth. It helps you feel safe in your own expression, which ultimately leads to you making choices that are more transparent, which in turn makes it simpler for you to achieve the objectives you have set for yourself in life without any reservations.

A lack of willpower and drive might be a symptom of the throat chakra being blocked. It causes feelings of powerlessness and inadequacy, which, along with the fact that it is difficult to articulate one's emotions and ideas, may become a burden. Some individuals develop eating disorders such as bulimia and anorexia nervosa as a consequence of bottling up their emotions within. Others generate a lot of conflict because they are quick to anger and don't give much consideration to the consequences of their actions before they leap into a situation.

6. The Chakra of the Third Eye

This chakra is connected to one's innate abilities as well as their imagination and perception. It makes use of the quality of light and functions as the energetic core from which you are able to access higher spiritual levels. Because it enables you to perceive all of the conditions in your environment, the third eye is considered to be the doorway to knowledge, wisdom, and the truth.

When one is meditating, dreaming, or manipulating the energy of the chakra, the third eye contributes to the process of bringing out inner knowledge in the form of visuals, colors, and sensations. This energy center is the ultimate power center for healing ourselves as well as others and having a better grasp of the world around us since it gives us the capacity to comprehend mental ideas and the ability to envision them.

When your third eye is opened and in a balanced state, you will see significant improvements in the areas of creativity, imagination, and instinct. Because of the third eye, it's possible that you'll start to feel or know things that aren't as fully formed.

If this chakra has grown more in this center than the others have, you may find that it is difficult for you to deal with things relating to everyday routines and even bodily concerns. If this chakra is powerful but dysfunctional, you may find yourself caught up in illusions and glamour, and you may even find yourself drawn to drugs in the hope that they may briefly offer you access to the world of your dreams.

If this energy center is blocked off, it may lead to a lack of creativity, a restricted imagination, and a lowered level of awareness; as a consequence, one's life will be of a lower quality in terms of higher direction. People who have a problem with their third eye tend to have little faith in anything that cannot be seen or touched. They find it difficult to be religious, and as a result, the vast majority of them do not believe in God or in life after death. They have a firm faith in things such as scientific knowledge, superficial interpretations, and intellectual capacity.

7. The third eye chakra

It is said that this chakra is the link that connects the physical body to the spiritual realm. It is the foundation upon which information, knowledge, and comprehension are built. It is associated to the pineal gland, which is involved in the management of the internal click of the body, and as a result, it is connected with ideas.

After having established a connection directly with a higher self, the crown chakra is said to be the source of respect, infinity, or wisdom as well as an insight that comes from a spiritual understanding, according to Eastern mystical beliefs. You are able to go to other energy realities, such as the sky, by connecting to a consciousness that extends beyond your own particular self and the material world via this energy center. You could even be able to obtain insights or other information from a higher existence via its use.

The insights that one receives are where extraordinary knowledge, religious experience, and higher intuition originate. These are the sources. You have the potential to be able to offer healing, unconditional love, and energy to every location in the universe by activating your crown chakra. This chakra represents the foundation for energy healing modalities such as therapeutic touch and Reiki, as well as the spiritual power of prayer. Grace, angels, immorality, and one's ability to engage with heavenly energies are all associated with the crown chakra.

It is essential to learn how to balance, cleanse, and heal your chakras after you have a better knowledge of chakras. This may be done by meditating on certain colors.

Meditation On The Heart Chakra

Place yourself on a level surface and lie down. Check that you are not experiencing any discomfort. Put a stop to your yawning.

Take a long, deep breath in, and then let it out gently. Repeat this a further two times.

After that, take a deep breath in and then wrap your arms around your body as if you were hugging yourself. In addition, when you exhale, extend your arms out to your sides and let them rest on the ground in front of you.

While you are lying on your back, let yourself to experience both the vulnerability you feel as a person as well as the connection you feel to the land.

Stay as calm as possible and take a couple more deep breaths, making sure to exhale gently each time.

Close your eyes and imagine that you are expelling all of the bad energy that you have been holding onto as you let out each breath.

Every time you let out an exhale, give yourself permission to release all of the negative energy that are holding you back, such as avarice, wrath, hatred, and envy.

And as you draw in air, picture good and fresh life energy streaming through your whole body.Do this as you inhale.

Pay attention to the cadence of your own breathing. The sound you hear is the rhythm of your heart pounding. Each and every beat is important because it brings fresh energy into your body. Every time your heart beats, you should be reminding yourself that you have the capacity to both give and receive love.

Relax both your physical self and your mental self.

The next time you take a breath in, let the love that is freely flowing all around you to enter your heart as you do so.

Send forth the love that you have and feel for the people around you as you let the breath out of your body.

Permit the feeling of love to permeate your whole body.

Stay lying down for the next several minutes. Make the most of this opportunity to rid your heart of all of the negative emotions like fear, rage, hatred, jealousy, and resentment.

Now, when you are ready, gently open your eyes, and share the love that you feel with your family, friends, and that one person who really stands out to you.

You should share the love that is in your heart with other people, as well as be open to receiving any love that is sent in your direction.

The Chakra of Your Third Eye

Your sixth chakra is known as Agnya, and it may be found in the centre of your forehead. This is where your conditioning and ego are stored. The Sun is the planet that bestows its influence over this chakra. Your very existence and the person you are are both controlled by the Sun. It has something to do with the energy that the Sun is a part of. This refers to your dominant astrological sign or planet. You will be able to get knowledge about the stage of your own progress no matter where it is situated. It tells where you are in the process of enlightenment or really comprehending something, and it also sheds light on the lessons that you need to learn in this lifetime. This chakra, together with this planet, contributes to the formation of your identity. Your identity and "who" you are are composed of a myriad of interconnected aspects. Because of this, your soul is completely distinct from all others. A variety of factors, such as the friends you keep, the education you get, your family, and other aspects of your life, may have an effect on who you are as an individual. The problem is that all of these identities are established via your ego, which presents a hurdle.

You are being conditioned by your ego. When you have access to your Third Eye, your ego will no longer be in charge. This is due to the fact that your Soul is capable of growing, which reveals your authentic self. You will develop more humility as you grow to understand your True Self. There is a possibility that you battle with your ego if the Sun is really powerful in your birth chart. It is not essential for you to be as selfish, pretentious, and dominant as you will be. It's also possible that you're vain. This sense of vanity might prevent your sixth chakra from functioning as it should. It is possible that you may acquire a feeling of superiority, which will cause you to become estranged from the people around you as well as from your Source. Because you are being directed and controlled by your ego, you do not disclose your True Self to others around you. When you are able to open it up and establish a connection with your Soul, you have an incredible opportunity to forgive. Because you are aware that everything that is inside you is also within everything else around you, you have a sense of connection to both your own Self and everything else around you.

Your third eye chakra.

Your Sahasrara, also known as your Crown Chakra, is the seventh and last major chakra. This rests on the very top of your head, either directly on top of the center of your skull or just above it. This is where there was a soft area when you were a newborn; the location where the skull bones had not yet solidified and closed over completely. The Moon is the planet that bestows its influence over this chakra. In astrology, the moon is considered to be the ruler of the sign Cancer. This chakra is located at the crown of the head and represents the culmination and synthesis of all of the other chakras. At this particular juncture, the energies and characteristics of all of the chakras come together. Your thoughts, your instincts, and your emotions are all involved in the administration of the Moon. When the Crown chakra is open or when it is flowing freely, it is simpler for all of the other chakras to cooperate with one another. In addition to this, it facilitates your connection with the vitality of the universe. Because of this profound connection, you go beyond only your own awareness. The position of the Moon in your birth chart is symbolic of the realm beyond conscious awareness and represents a state that is constantly present. It exerts its authority over the whole cosmos.

This indicates that when your Crown is open and flowing, your awareness is linked to the intellect or consciousness of the whole universe. You are spiritual, self-sacrificing, creative, instinctive, and sensitive if your birth chart reveals a high presence of the Moon. The Moon has a nurturing and creative energy about it. It fosters the feeling of being a mother or someone who cares for others while also representing such feeling. Since the Moon completes one round around the zodiac quicker than any other planet, its characteristics are subject to ongoing change. Your personality will shift as a direct result of this alteration. Alteration is one thing that will never stop occurring in your life. This indicates that you have a good capacity to adjust fast and readily to the majority of different situations and circumstances. Because of this, you will benefit from the constant change that the universe experiences. When you have a strong connection to the Moon and this chakra is open, you experience the sensation of being a single drop that has been blended inconspicuously into the whole of the ocean, ebbing and flowing in unison with the collective as the collective.

www.ingramcontent.com/pod-product-compliance
Lightning Source LLC
Chambersburg PA
CBHW050239120526
44590CB00016B/2152